CHESAPEAKE

D1262316

Lee Blessing

BROADWAY PLAY PUBLISHING INC
56 E 81st St., NY NY 10028-0202
212 772-8334 fax: 212 772-8358
http://www.BroadwayPlayPubl.com

CHESAPEAKE
© Copyright 2000 by Lee Blessing

First printing: December 2000
I S B N: 0-88145-179-7

Book design: Marie Donovan
Word processing: Microsoft Word for Windows
Typographic controls: Xerox Ventura Publisher 2.0 P E
Typeface: Palatino
Copy editing: Michele Travis
Printed on recycled acid-free paper and bound in the
U S A

CONTENTS

ABOUT THE AUTHOR

New York's Signature Theater devoted its second season to Lee Blessing's work, including the world premiere of PATIENT A. Blessing's A WALK IN THE WOODS ran on Broadway; the production later toured to Moscow. It was also seen in London's West End, starring Sir Alec Guinness, and on P B S's *American Playhouse*. His plays have been nominated for the Tony and Olivier Awards as well as the Pulitzer Prize, have premiered at the Manhattan Theater Club, Yale Repertory Theater, La Jolla Playhouse and Actors Theater of Louisville, among others. Awards include the American Theater Critics Award, the George and Elisabeth Maron Award and the L A Drama Critics Circle Award (for his widely produced ELEEMOSYNARY). Blessing has received grants from the N E A as well as the Guggenheim, Bush, McKnight, and Jerome Foundations. Heinemann has published two collections of his work. Blessing's T N T film *Cooperstown*, starring Alan Arkin and Graham Greene, won the Humanitas Prize and three Cable Ace nominations, including best screenplay. With collaborator Jeanne Blake he's written for *Homicide: Life on the Street*, *Picket Fences* and *Nothing Sacred*, as well as the Andrew Davis feature film *Steal Big, Steal Little*.

ORIGINAL PRODUCTION

CHESAPEAKE was originally presented by New York Stage and Film Company (Mark Linn-Baker, Max Mayer, Leslie Urdang—Producing Directors; Johanna Pfaelzer—Managing Producer) and The Powerhouse Theater at Vassar in June 1999.

CHESAPEAKE was subsequently produced Off-Broadway by James B Freydberg, William P Suter, and Susann Brinkley; Steven Chaikelson, Gary R Marano, and Michael Woods, Associate Producers in association with Second Stage Theater. The cast and creative contributors were:

KERR . . . . Mark Linn-Baker

Director . . . . Max Mayer
Set designer . . . . Adrianne Lobel
Costume designer .Susan Hilferty
Lighting designer . . . . James F Ingalls
Sound designer . . . . Darron L West
Production stage manager . . . .Laura Brown MacKinnon
Production manager . . . . Kai Brothers

The author wishes to express his deepest thanks to everyone involved in the play's original production, and in particular to Mark Linn-Baker for his inspired performance.

for Jeanne

The wise old men of India say,

"If you loved your dog too much,
in your next life you'll be a dog—
yet full of human memories."

Sujata Bhatt, 1983

ACT ONE

(Lights bump from black to full, to reveal KERR, *alone center. As* KERR *starts to speak, a dog barks offstage.* KERR *freezes, then listens for another bark. None comes.)*

*(*KERR's *mouth opens again. Again the dog barks.* KERR's *head jerks in that direction. Silence. To the audience)*

KERR: You didn't...hear anything, did you?

(A long bout of barking. KERR *winces with a deep, familiar pain. Finally the dog stops.)*

KERR: In 1807—

*(*KERR *opens his mouth once more. No bark this time, but he gives a look anyway)*

KERR: In 1807, a ship loaded with cod from the fisheries of Newfoundland sailed into Chesapeake Bay and, well...sank. The entire crew was rescued—plus two dogs. No one remembers the name of that ship, or any of the crew. The dogs however, were named Sailor and Canton.

(The dog barks once. KERR's *head swings, bird dog-like, in that direction. To audience)*

KERR: Sailor was a Newfoundland water dog. Canton was a female of the same breed. These weren't the fluffy Saint Bernard-like dogs we call Newfoundlands today. They were more like black Labs. Most important, they were the ancestors of the Chesapeake Bay Retriever.

(A loud, crisp bark. KERR stares in its direction, bristling with frustrated malevolence, then works for self-control, giving the audience an embarrassed grin.)

KERR: What you're listening to is my dream—

(Steady barking. KERR tries to talk over it.)

KERR: *My repeating dream. I had it every night for over a—*

(The dog stops.)

KERR: For over a year. The dog is, of course, a Chesapeake Bay Retriever. Proud descendant of Sailor and Canton and whatever dogs or bitches happened to be nearby. Some say Canton was tied to a tree in a swamp and there mated to an otter. Perverse notion, but it would explain their strong swimming.

(The dog starts barking again.)

KERR: *The Chesapeake Bay Retriever—or Chessie, as I refuse to call it—is one of the earliest examples of a genuinely American breed.*

(The dog stops)

KERR: It's not the prettiest of dogs, it's not the friendliest—

(Another, rather dangerous bark)

KERR: And it's certainly not the most popular. It is, however, the finest retriever in the world. No creature on Earth feels more natural with a duck in its mouth.

(A friendly little woof. KERR stares angrily in that direction.)

KERR: This wasn't just some dog-next-door, by the way. No, this was a far more serious dog. This was a yellow-eyed, oily coated, Necco-wafer-colored e-mail from hell that slipped from the T V screen directly into my hypothalamus and took over my autonomic nervous system. This dog barked *inside* me.

*(A flurry of barking, which crescendoes and distorts.
KERR actually begins to writhe in pain, slowly crumpling
into the fetal position until the barking finally stops. Silence)*

KERR: So. Who was this unremitting pooch of the
airwaves, or as I called him: death's pet? None other
than the most prized possession of Representative
Therm Pooley, congressman from my home district—
or what used to be my home. Pooley's dog was at
his side for every sound-bite and commercial—there
to transform ribbon-cuttings into ribbon chewings,
shake paws with all the reporters and lick every baby.

(The dog whines, eliciting a reflexive shudder from KERR.)

KERR: The registered name of this beast was Lord
Ratliff of Luckymore. On the campaign trail he was
always Lucky. In private, the congressman referred
to him simply as Rat.

I suppose it's inappropriate to feel embarrassment for
an entire region of the country, still that's the emotion
I had listening as a young, Southern bisexual to Therm
Pooley's standard campaign speech. In it, he suggested
that since the federal government refused to classify
homosexuality as a disease, it should go ahead and
tax gays for their high-risk lifestyle. Such enlightened
views won him several landslides—and won me the
realization that I needed to *move north*.

I went to New York. I was miserable, alone, barely
creeping out of the closet, yet I felt freer than I'd
ever been. I got work in a bookstore, started dating
waitresses—and waiters—and began for the first time
to pursue a dream I'd had since childhood. A perfectly
natural ambition —not that I could mention it in my
home town.

(More barking from offstage)

KERR: *Quiet!*

(A dog's whimper. To audience)

KERR: I don't suppose many of you have displayed
your genitalia in public. My dream—to become a
performance artist—has afforded me that particular
privilege. My name is Kerr. Maybe you've heard of
me? I didn't think so. Anyway—

I first discovered my life's passion when I was ten.
My father took me to an art museum. He wasn't an
educated man—not even a bright man. But he was
stuck with me one rainy afternoon, so...

Like refugees from a disaster we couldn't quite
remember, we trudged through Greek and Roman
statuary, Renaissance tapestries, Dutch landscapes.
At each piece my father would stop and stare dutifully,
and give a soft, unconscious sigh of utter capitulation—
as though saying, "There it is. There it is."—not
knowing for the life of him what "it" was. Exactly
seven seconds in front of each work, each unit of
culture, then on to the next. Seven seconds. My father
assumed if you go to a museum, you're there to see
everything, otherwise you might have to come back.

Durer, Velasquez, Monet—it never occurred to him to
skip a painting. Or a wall, or a whole gallery. He could
not understand art, yet he would give it to me. It was
worse with the Moderns. The works were just flat
surfaces now, disfigured with paint. Unappealing,
aggressive, disturbingly sexual. Was that a breast?
Or merely a shape designed to trap him into an
excitement for which he could find no name?

"There it is. There it is." *What?*

At last we stood at the museum's open front door.
The sun hung in the wet trees like a bullseye.
A nervous young man tapped my father on the arm.

"Aren't you staying for the performance? In the small
auditorium? It's just about to start".

There were five of us, including the performer—a man
with smooth skin and a white pompadour. He wore a
tuxedo. On the floor to his left was a heavy, black frying
pan. To his right, a sturdy wooden spoon. Behind him a
sign read: "ONE THOUSAND EVEN BEATS ON THE
FRYING PAN."

My father stared straight ahead. Clearly, he'd decided
to endure whatever must be endured to baptize me
fully in the dark, repellent waters of art. The performer
never spoke. He picked up the tools of his...trade?...held
the frying pan like a miniature cello and struck it once,
sharply. The room filled with a dull, not-very-resonant
tone.

(Beats like those described are heard.)

KERR: Exactly seven seconds later he struck the frying
pan again—and every seven seconds after
that—without variation.

(The beats continue.)

KERR: It dawned on us that he was entirely serious
about hitting this pan one thousand times while we
sat there. I looked at the rest of the audience: a confused-
looking Asian couple, in their eighties maybe?

At the half-hour mark, the old couple began to
complain loudly in Chinese. It didn't bother the
frying-pan virtuoso. On he went, nuzzled against the
enfolding stillness between each of his never-ending
beats. I was ready to leave at the slightest sign from
my father. Like a schooling fish, poised to turn in
any direction—toward the door, perhaps?

Finally the Chinese man tried to storm the stage.
His wife grabbed his arm, pleading as he dragged
her step by step toward the performer. Inches away,

the old man shouted what must have been a horrible insult—in Chinese—and stalked out. His wife bowed and followed.

The beats never varied; my father never moved. At exactly one hour, or five hundred and sixteen beats—as I'd had more than enough time to calculate—my father began to cry. He was not just trying to endure this tiny bubble of aesthetic sadism, he was trying to enjoy it. And I saw that art was a test, plain and simple. Not an intellectual test—a spiritual one. Instinctively my father knew if he could sit through this performance— arguably the worst art in the world—then he would stand on a particular and distant shore with those who saw that even failed art is better than no art at all. And he would stand there with his own child. For the first—and only— time, I saw my father as a hero.

(The beats continue.)

KERR: Imagine. Aching to participate fully in... *this.* That's when I knew that art is not an act of communication—
that's just what people say when they want grant money. No. Art is an act of will—like crime or law or religion. A form of domination, benevolent maybe, but domination all the same. And I knew one more thing. I knew if art could do that to my father, even once, that I would be an artist forever.

(The final beat, then silence)

KERR: But as I grew up, I realized it wasn't just art I'd fallen in love with. Sure, art was there to confront all the smugness and unoriginality in society, to upset everybody's applecart. But upsetting the applecart of art—that's what I was after. I dreamed of people entering theatres, not knowing what might happen— knowing only that all their expectations would be assaulted. I dreamed, not of entertaining an audience, but of attacking it. And I dreamed of audiences heroic enough to survive.

(Excitedly) There was a world of precedents. I went back over a hundred years to *Ubu Roi*, the Futurists—all of it. The Futurists were the best. In the early 1900s a man named Filippo Marinetti published a manifesto called Futurism. He was terrified the new century would continue all the stultifying habits of the last. And why not? In his world people listened to Verdi and Puccini like so many bobbing-head dolls. Everyone knew where to laugh and where to cry. Disaster.

So he and a few buddies would stand in cafés wearing funnels on their bodies and cones on their heads and spout poems that made no sense at all—not even real words sometimes— *(Suddenly reciting and stomping around like Frankenstein's monster)* "Bulubu bulu bulu bulu bulu bulu—"

It was great! Know what they liked best? Being booed. Twenty different poets would recite at the same time. They'd piss on each other's paintings, right on stage. They'd insult the audience; they'd put glue on the seats—anything to get a reaction. When people threw potatoes, the Futurists would dare them to come up and fight! Any performance that didn't result in jail was a failure!

For the Futurists, art had to hurt, frighten—or who could take it seriously? They wrote plays for actors' *feet*. They wrote one with only a dog in it, called *There Is No Dog*. Concerts of machine and traffic noises, broadcast from planes before it was safe to go up in planes. They risked their lives so that something, anything, in the new century would be different. "Thanks to us," Marinetti wrote, "life will no longer be a simple matter of bread and labor, but a *work of art*". That's what I wanted. To live not a life, but a work of art.

(Vigorous barking offstage. An echo effect as it subsides.
KERR's *head shakes dolefully.)*

KERR: How can you explain something like that to the
Therm Pooleys of the world? You can't. You just try to
pretend he doesn't exist. But how? He opposed federal
spending on AIDS, defense cuts, affirmative action,
gays in the military, gays in the schools, gays on Earth.
Everyone in the bookstore knew where I was from.
"He's your congressman, why don't you do
something?"

Every day I heard it. And every night I performed.
The act I created was political, but I avoided all mention
of Therm Pooley— which only made things worse.
Friends actually shunned me. Or they'd say, "Therm
Pooley has worked every waking hour for the complete
destruction of the National Endowment for the Arts".

(Angrily) It wasn't my fault! I'd moved—a thousand
miles! I didn't *have* to care; why should I? Don't ask,
don't tell. Don't read, don't learn, don't fulminate
with bottled-up rage— I could forget Therm Pooley!

(A bark. KERR *stares balefully.)*

KERR: But that dog.

Pooley had an assistant—a twenty-one-year-old
fundamentalist named Stacey. She carried a Frisbee
so Therm could wow the press at any time with the
acrobatics of good, ol' Lucky.

"Look at that boy jump! Trained him myself,"
Therm would chuckle as the Rat-dog capered.
A leaping, quivering object, eternal photo-op
magnet. A politician's very, *very* best friend.

Then came a year—I think it was the Year of the
Rat—when our fates were linked finally and forever.
At nearly the same moment, I was awarded a grant
by the N E A, and Therm Pooley declared himself a

candidate for the U S Senate. He faced a tough,
state-wide race, and was looking for any advantage.
When informed I was a product of his own district,
Pooley tried to get my grant revoked—on the grounds,
he said, of obscenity.

(With disdain) Obscenity. I won't describe my entire act.
It was perhaps no "Thousand Even Beats" but a very
high level of moral and artistic quality was involved.
The part of my act he cited involved a reading from
the Bible—specifically, Solomon's Song.

Solomon, you may recall, was allowed to celebrate an
adoration of, and lust for, the human form. It's a long,
dry march from the oasis of Solomon's Song to any
comparable passage in world religion. So I thought I'd
help fill a few spiritual canteens, as it were, by reading
the beautiful little thing out loud. And because theater
is showing, as I read I made sure to remove all my
clothes.

Not in any lurid way. I didn't even remove the clothes
myself. I had the audience do it. They came up, one at a
time, and divested me of one—only one to a customer,
that was my rule—piece of clothing: shoe, sock, jacket...
whatever. I always wore as many clothes as there were
members of the audience. Some nights that was almost
a hundred garments. It made me look like I should be
sorted in the back of Goodwill—still it's what I wore.

(Remembering with a smile, over ethereal music)

KERR: "A bundle of myrrh is my well-beloved unto me;
he shall lie all night betwixt my breasts." And on it
goes: "Thy navel is like a round goblet..." "Thy
belly...like an heap of wheat set about with lilies."

(The music fades out.)

KERR: It's not the lust that embarrasses us, it's the
luxury. The relentless comparison with jewels, animals,

crops—all those symbols of wealth and immortality.
How can we be that good, that valuable? Gold endures,
but the body... We paint it, worry over it, smother it
with clothes. We pray others will lust after it, even as
it fills us with secret disgust. And of course we hate it,
because it must inevitably welcome disease, infestation
and death. Where is the body? In an early grave, buried
in our clothes. And Lazarus-like, I ask the audience to
roll away the stone of their fear—disrobe me, even as I
sing not my, but God's, praises of this most magisterial
of all parlor tricks, this moment of flesh set between
two ages of dust.

(As the music begins again)

KERR: "Honey and milk are under thy tongue..."
"The smell of thy nose like apples."

And they did come up. Someone would always skitter
forth and pluck the outermost coat or glove—or hat.
Slowly the rest would follow. In the end I stood buck
naked, they themselves had made me so, and it was not
Las Vegas or some Times Square peepshow, it was art.

"Open to me...my love, my dove, my undefiled: for my
head is filled with dew, and my locks with the drops of
the night."

(With a satisfied sigh, as the music fades)

KERR: It was a wonderful piece. I never felt more
essentially beautiful than in those moments. And of
course, I made sure the lighting was very flattering.

Yet all would-be Senator Pooley saw was prurience.
How? The text was from the mouth of the Almighty.
No children were allowed. No one quivered with lust.
Not a single orgasm was ever achieved.

All right, there was one. But I'm sure it was a fake. As I
stood onstage in all my glory—applause cascading—
someone in the back row suddenly reached a mystical

point of no return and plunged over love's Niagara
right in front of God and everybody. I remember
thinking how Signore Marinetti would have enjoyed
that moment. The patron, at whom I never got a
good look, rushed out—in misplaced embarrassment,
I thought. It wasn't till the next day I realized what had
transpired. A critic for the Bergen County *Patriot* had
come by that night and "just happened" to catch our
little moment of added excitement. From there the story
went everywhere—two weeks before election day.

What Therm Pooley had done was obvious: plant
a groaner in the last row, add a reporter and *voila*!
Instant campaign fodder. I was an advocate of sex
in public places, purveyor of filth disguised as art—
and I *had a grant.*

(In a strong, righteous drawl) "Po-or-nog-raphy!!
Po-or-NOG-raphy!!!" The word welled out of
Therm Pooley from an incalculable depth of
mythic resentment. Suddenly my performance
represented every outrage the South had ever borne.
"Po-or-nog-raphy!" That was why the South had lost
the Civil War. He purposely mispronounced the first
syllable— "Po-or"—to suggest, I suppose, that a
single orgasm was responsible for all the poverty
in Appalachia.

Over and over he said it, and always with his family
and Lucky the Hellhound by his side, standing against
the flood of perversity—oh, you know the speech.
And you know where it plays. Pooley's numbers
went up three points overnight, five in a week.

C N N phoned to get my reaction to what the *Post* was
calling the "comer and the critic". Reporters sent me
tapes of Pooley's new commercials. They all ended
with the same ritual question: *(In a broad drawl)*
"Lucky, you're an animal. Would you behave like
that?" And Lucky would give a little lost whimper—

(Such whimpering comes.)

KERR: And in a tight close-up, they would attribute
moral values to a dog. Ol' Lucky boy would lie down
and put his forepaws over his eyes, just like Petey in
the "Our Gang" comedies—

(Suddenly flaring)

KERR: I mean who's *running* this country!!? Who's—!!?
(Recomposing himself) I wanted to defend myself, but
every time I opened my mouth, nothing came out.
Every night I woke in a dead sweat from the same
nightmare: Pooley's dog, the Lord of Rats, barking
insanely on my chest, fangs bared, his drool pooling
into the little hollow at the base of my throat.

He won by two percentage points. *Time* called it the
most stunning performance piece of the year—meaning
Pooley, not me. C N N called one last time. "Anything
to say?" "No," I whispered, and hung up. For a week
I sat alone in my apartment. Then I got a call.

A man invited me for a drink. He wouldn't give his
name, just said I'd be interested. We met in a hotel bar.
The man said he worked for Therm Pooley, said the
Senator-elect wanted to meet me face to face. Would
I care to go upstairs? *(Sighing)* Why do we always go
upstairs? "Hitler's upstairs. Want to meet him?" "O K".
I was shown to a room and left alone. After a few
minutes, Therm Pooley walked in with a big smile.
"Don't talk; just listen," he said.

"I'm not here. I'm not even in New York. Right now
I'm at my country place outside D C, being the kind of
husband and father this nation needs more of. I have
seventeen people who will swear to that fact. Is that
understood?"

I nodded.

"First, I want to thank you for my election. Second,
I'm glad I used you shamelessly during the campaign.
Like most artists, you're an overgrown baby addicted
to sucking the tit of a tired America. Besides, I gave you
more free publicity than you could buy in a year. Third,
I won't be going after your ill-deserved grant money.
And you can bank on the N E A surviving for awhile.
It was made in heaven to beat liberals over the head
with."

"One complaint I do have. What's all this garbage
about you not talking to C N N? You almost lost me
the election with that silent bit. Made me start to worry
about your mental health. You do have mental health?"

I nodded.

"As a token of my gratitude, in a few weeks a man
with no traceable connection to me will offer you a tour
of liberal northern cities, places even you can't harm.
I pay my debts, Kerr. You've earned it. Do me a favor,
though—learn what in hell the media's for."

He left. I couldn't believe it. Imagine how Marinetti
would have responded to this kind of co-option!
Of course, a tour would be nice, but—no. *No!!*
Pooley'd left my grant in place? Fine. It would
fund my new project.

But...what would my project be?

(Sudden hearty, unfriendly barking offstage)

KERR: It was so easy. Lucky—the political knick-knack,
pet of my bête noir. How much, I wondered, would a
dognapping really cost?

(The dog gives a low, plaintive howl. KERR's *excitement
grows.)*

KERR: The very thought was so liberating! Real-life
protest. That's the trouble with artists. We're too busy

performing sublimated protest ever to do the real thing.
Miners, students, farmers put their lives on the line,
fight the National Guard! What do we do? Create
pitiful, symbolic gestures: "The Day Without Art".
"Golly—guess we'll have to wait *till tomorrow*."

That was going to stop with me.

(As the dog begins to growl softly)

KERR: I would grab this dog and humiliate Therm
Pooley as he had humiliated me.

(The growl stops with the sound of snapping jaws.)

KERR: I swore on the grave of Filippo Marinetti that I
would do anything, *give my life if necessary*, to humble
that man.

I estimated the hours in the library, hardware store, pet
store, hi-tech specialty shops. I calculated the number of
weeks required, the price of used minivans, gas, food,
etc. I researched the cost of animal tranquilizers and the
cost of a gun. The entire project came to exactly four
dollars and eight cents over the amount of my grant.
Since it was art, I sprang for the difference. The aim was
not just to steal his dog, but to transform the animal—
to shift its loyalty from Pooley to me. Where would I
accomplish this? Chesapeake Bay. Yes, Lord Ratliff of
Fucking Luckymore was going home—home to guard
a remote fishing shack.

I'd return him to his roots. I'd train him in the ways of
the oyster, the duck and the clam—I'd learn these ways
first, then I'd train him. In the end, I'd have a dog who
loved me, not Therm Pooley.

And since it was a government-funded project, there
was an even greater goal: to record the entire thing on
video, especially the part where I returned the mutt,
in secret and completely unharmed. I'd make it the
centerpiece of my next show. Then and only then, on

opening night, would the world know what I had done.
The only paper I'd invite would be the Bergen County
Patriot. Special engraved invitations would be hand-
delivered to Senator Pooley and the head of the
N E A. This vision felt pure.

(Picking up a glass of water) Oh sure, prison time was
a strong likelihood. *(He drinks)* But I'd be a first-time
offender. And jail never stopped Marinetti.

(Sound of a woman's laughter, and a dog at play)

KERR: Thus I found myself sitting across from the
apartment of Pooley's luminous assistant, Stacey.
There, two nights a month, Lucky stayed at the home
of the beautiful, young fundamentalist. On the seat
of my minivan was a black hood, a stick-and-collar
arrangement for the control of dangerous animals,
a muzzle, the business end of a Louisville Slugger—
and a video recorder I called Rat-cam. I wore a white
jumpsuit complete with the name "Frankie." The back
of the van was caged in. On my lap was a small-caliber
pistol which fired a tiny hypodermic filled with a
compound you and I might really enjoy.

Every morning Stacey gunned her car down the quiet,
tree-lined street. Every evening after a long day
wrangling the senatorial pooch, she'd crawl back.

Something haunted me about Stacey's face. I stared
and stared from across the street, but I couldn't...
And suddenly I knew! She was an exact double for
Valentine de Saint-Point!

(Soft music—Debussy or Satie)

KERR: She was a Futurist—like Marinetti. But one of
the very few women. God, she was beautiful! She
performed *The Manifesto of Lust* in 1913. It had poems
of love, poems of war—and my favorite, poems of
atmosphere. While she danced, mathematical equations

were projected on the walls. Debussy and Satie did
the music—it was a very big deal. *And* it was the
only Futurist performance ever to come to New York.
She was as American as Futurism ever got.

Now here she was again. I was mesmerized. I know it's
a bad dognapper who becomes involved in this way,
but what was I supposed to do? The image of Valentine
de Saint-Point floated before me every evening.
I started dreaming about her. What a relief! At last
I wasn't dreaming about you-know-who.

(A series of sharp barks vanquishes the music. KERR *groans)*

KERR: Finally Stacey brought Lucky home. I'd have
my chance in the morning. She always left at seven
forty-five. The moment she pulled out, I donned my
black hood, tucked the sawed-off baseball bat under
my arm and grabbed my Camcorder. I patted the gun
in my lap. She slowed at the corner. I rammed the van
into her path and jumped out. I waved the camera and
my gun with its hypodermic warhead in her face.

"Get out of the car!" I shouted. Rat-bastard was barking
his fucking head off, of course. I got a few shots of him
with the camera; I'd have to wait till he was outside for
the hypo.

"What do you want?!" *"Shut up! Get out!!"*

"Who *are* you?!"

"I'm Frankie!" I said, stabbing at my name patch.
"Can't you read?!" I tried to get her door open
and avoid Lucky's fangs at the same time.

"Frankie who? Why've you got a camera?!"

"Shut up!! Get out!!

"You're not Frankie. I've heard that voice."

"Get out!! Bring the *dog!"*

"Why do you want Lucky?"

"Just do it, bitch!"

I'd read that words like that instilled fear during a dogjacking. But God, she was so insulted. I felt like a criminal. I pointed the gun. Maybe I could get a shot.

"What are you *DOING!?*"

"SHUT UP!! " As I started to pull the trigger, she grabbed my arm. The needle shot through my boot—directly into my middle toe.

"*DAMN!*" I yelled. I stepped back, brandishing the bat.

"You were gonna shoot him!"

"IT'S A HYPO, DAMN IT!!

Her mouth fell open. "I know you! I know that voice. You're that Kerr person. I saw a tape. You're that...that *artist!*" I don't think I've ever heard the word "artist" spoken with as much contempt. I called her bitch; she called me artist. Marinetti would have loved it.

"Shut up!! Put this on him!" I handed her the stick-and-collar. Lucky growled, but Stacey talked to him a little-girlish sort of way, and he calmed down. As she slipped it on him, I pulled the dart out of my toe. She dragged Lucky out and offered me the stick.

"Muzzle him".

She did as she was told, whispering encouragement to the nervous retriever.

"Move away," I said.

"We'll find you, Lucky—don't worry. We know this person."

"MOVE AWAY!!

I grabbed the stick and started hauling Lucky into the van. But as I opened the door, Stacey's hand shot

forward and undid the muzzle. Gleefully, Lord of the
Rats lunged. I tried to hold him off, but the stick slipped
in my sweaty hand, and he buried his teeth deep in
my calf. I screamed and tried to shake him off. Stacey
swung at me with my own muzzle. The buckle drew
blood. That, by the way, is how you know you're taken
with a woman. If she remains attractive while she's
whipping your head with a buckle.

Finally I regained control of the stick and forced the
four-legged vampire into my van. As Stacey kept
swinging, I staggered to the front and heaved myself
in. She whipped the window. "He'll eat you alive!
You better give up now!" She looked magnificent.

I slammed it into drive and pulled away. I ripped off
the sweat-soaked hood. I was committed now. And it
felt good—except for the open wound in my leg, the
numbness in my foot and the fear placed in every cell
of my body by Lucky's growl, inches from the ear he
wanted so deeply to Van Gogh.

Now that I'd been 'made', as they say on the cop show
that's so much like that other cop show, I switched
to Plan B. I headed for the mountains of Virginia.
A couple nights up there and I could sneak back down
to my fully provisioned shack on the Chesapeake.

(Sound of loud barking)

KERR: Lucky started barking at the back of the van.
I looked in the mirror and saw Stacey's car. She was
following me! I sped up. Stacey sped up. My leg bled.
In the distance, the mountains loomed. I didn't know
where I was going. The roads coiled like snakes.

We headed into a public reserve—forest everywhere.
A wave of fatigue swept over me. I nearly went off the
road. Dirt and gravel sprayed everywhere. I looked
back to see Stacey's car punch through the wall of dust
I'd made. I roared around a corner and cut a hard right

down an almost unnoticeable dirt road. I looked
back—did she see me? Suddenly I was overcome
with the strangest sensation. Even though nearly
everything had gone wrong and I was filled with
animal tranquilizer and chasing over a rock-strewn
folly of a road, even though all these things were true,
I had never felt so exhilarated—no, so fulfilled—in my
entire life.

It was *better* that she knew who I was. This was my
response to Pooley's "jes' folks, man-with-his-dog"
routine. I trained the Camcorder on Lucky. See
America? See my simple, elegant solution? *Take away
the dog.* Deny the magician his card trick, and a nation
of idiot infants just one of their multitude of pacifiers.

I drove and taped. It was like a dream. My statement
was made. Failure was no longer possible. Nothing
could hurt me now. I hurtled over a rise, directly into
a fallen tree.

(Sound of a sickening, mid-forest crash)

KERR: The minivan was totaled. A deep gash blossomed
over my brow. Lord Ratliff wasn't even knocked off his
feet.

Stacey's car came over the rise. I tried to wipe the blood
off my face. I wanted her to see I was all right.

"Lucky! Lucky!!? Where's the dog!!!?

Where's the dog. Where do you think? In the van,
unhurt, master of all he surveys—master of your *heart*,
for God's—! I didn't actually say this. It came out more
like...well, gibberish.

She clawed at the jammed side door. Inside, the
unkillable Rat barked happily. I was on automatic
pilot now, shuffling away from the van, looking for
a place to lie down.

(The lapping sound of water. KERR *looks down.)*

KERR: And suddenly I noticed the reservoir. I was waist-deep in it actually, and it was more like a lake. No retaining wall—at least nothing had retained me.

The blood running down my face was coming faster. I thought it must look like a veil, the kind Valentine de Saint-Point wore while she danced. My new look; maybe I could put it in my act. I heard one last distant bark from the joyous Rat.

(A distant bark)

KERR: And I sank into the still, cold water as gently as two lovers sink together, or as two strange and wonderful animals sniff each other's velvet muzzles, or as once—and far too often—I would sink into the silence of a performance for which no tickets had been sold.

Most bodies float. Mine doesn't. I don't know if the density of performance artists is greater than the general population, or if it's just personal, but the direction my body moves in water is always straight down, as though I know instinctively that true transcendence takes us not up but down: into the pipes, the sewers, the bay—where we are not so much dissolved as solved. And the answer to the mystery of our lives is: more lives. More and more. A bay full. An ocean—

And that's when I felt the teeth. Those same teeth that had so enjoyed their recent stay in my calf. But now they weren't biting. They were...arranging, moving my tangled sleeve around until they could take a good grip and start to pull. Up I came, barely conscious, yet I knew what was happening. The ultimate humiliation: being saved from drowning by Lord Ratliff of Luckymore, dog hero, an animal so deficient in intelligence he ran right past the warm arms of a loving

woman and into this cold water on a mission of pure
instinct whose one-word message he could never resist:
retrieve. Retrieve anything. Duck, decoy, rotting apple,
piece of garbage, performance artist. Tomorrow his
vacant canine smile will stare from all the papers as
Therm Pooley graciously pardons my mad, pathetic
attempt at crime—while at the same time calling for
repayment of the grant I've so recklessly squandered.

When our heads broke the surface Stacey yelled,
"Lucky! Are you all right? Come out of there!"
We'd drifted in some sort of current and emerged by
a giant concrete ramp that led onto a broad sort of pier.
I held Lucky's collar. The irony was not lost on Stacey.
"He's good enough to save your life, I see." She had
the Camcorder. She was taping it all: evidence for the
Senator?

I tried to speak, but a coughing fit made it impossible.
And it's a point of some regret, because just then
Lucky shook water out of his coat. I stepped back,
but my hand was caught under his collar. I slipped
and couldn't help but pull Lucky after me. We tumbled
over the far edge of the pier.

In my half-drowned state, I'd failed to notice a
pertinent fact—the pier on which we stood was part
of an enormous dam. On one side lay the reservoir.
On the other...two hundred unimpeded feet of the
finest air in all Virginia.

Of course, if this were a movie you'd know what comes
next. Lucky or I would catch a branch or root—or the
rusty-but-reliable end of an iron reinforcing rod—and
we'd cheat death in the most exciting way possible.
I would live because I'm the protagonist. Lucky would
live because he's a dog.

But this is not a movie; this is performance art. And this
is why you hate it. And fear it. Because for us there was

no branch, no root, no rod of iron. Only a dazed, absurd
fall from the helpless grace of life all the way down to
its stony opposite. I wish I could say I died like a dog,
but that was Lucky's privilege. Fortunately death—
which is a kind of trauma—tends to erase short-term
memory. Thus I have no clear recollection of the shouts,
barks, vain graspings—recriminating looks?—which
presumably accompanied our fall.

Did I spend my last moments staring back up at
the fast-disappearing image of the horrified, angelic
Stacey? Was she still taping? Did I gaze sheepishly at
a dog who knew we were both in trouble, but was still
vague on how much? What, finally, would it matter?
My act would stand for what it was: a real protest,
however clumsy. Precisely what I'd meant to say was
lost, but the raw act was there; everyone would know—
a precious few might understand. And at least I'd never
again be forced to endure a culture that may as well sit
in a continent-sized petri dish.

After all, it doesn't take a career in the theater to know
that behind the asbestos fire-curtain of death there are
no encores. At least, that's what I thought.

(*Offstage, the sound of puppies whining. Fade to black*)

END OF ACT ONE

ACT TWO

(Darkness. Low sound of a vehicle speeding along)

KERR: I woke up in a vehicle of some kind. I thought it might be an ambulance, but an ambulance would have lights, sounds, clicks and bongs. And wouldn't there be a siren? But there was just this speeding along, in utter darkness.

Something in front of me had the most peculiar smell. Not a bad smell, just...odd. I sniffed again. It smelled incredibly familiar, yet I couldn't place it. I stuck my tongue out and touched it, you know, lightly. I almost had it. I almost knew...

I licked it, tentatively, a couple times. I still didn't know what it was. Just then a semi passed us, and in its lights I could see what I'd been licking: it was my penis.

(Doppler effect of a semi roaring by. A light wipes across the surprised face of KERR. *As he continues, lights fade up)*

KERR: Jesus Christ! *Was* it a penis?! It couldn't have been. What was going on?! I couldn't see a thing. My heart was racing. My *heart*?! How could it even be beating?! I couldn't be alive. Nothing could have survived that fall. Desperately, I tried to think what my patron saint, Filippo Marinetti, would do in this situation. But what on Earth was the situation?

We turned onto a loud, bumpy road and stopped. There were voices in back. I couldn't see anyone, but then...and this is one of the oddest sensations

I ever had—I could *smell* them. Even though they were outside the vehicle. They all smelled different. I could actually tell how many there were.

Suddenly a gate in back was thrown down. I was blinded by the rays of the rising sun. A man spoke. (*In a rural Southern voice*) "How you doin' in there, boy? Come out of it yet?" (*Tentatively*) O K—O K, it could be Hell. Hell could smell like a farm. It could have a Southern accent.

The voice spoke again, this time to the others. "Don't worry—he'll be fine."

Then I heard three words that froze my heart.

"What's his name?"

I squinted into the sun; I couldn't see their faces. I took a big whiff and—*my God!* I could smell him—clear as day! Therm Pooley!

I heard a woman's voice—one I didn't recognize. "No, Sammy, don't tell us. We don't want it in our heads."

Why's Therm Pooley here?! He didn't die, I did! I tried to say something, but somehow I couldn't.

The woman barked a command: "Get up!"

Instantly I got to my feet... (*Looking down with an onrush of horror*) All... FOUR OF THEM?!!

And then I was spinning, clattering, barking—BARKING?!! A firm hand reached in and hauled me by the collar—COLLAR!!—out into the cold, inhuman light of dawn. I was staring at knees. My tongue seemed to be falling out of my mouth. I was... (*In a horrified whisper*) I was covered with hair—!!!

The woman grabbed me by the jaw and stared straight in my eye. "Lucky—that's your name. Lord Ratliff of Luckymore."

The other woman spoke. "Amazing. He looks just like him." It was Stacey. Automatically, I wagged my tail— *(In a piteous tone) Tail—!?*

"He oughta," said Sammy. "Same litter".

The first woman's face loomed. "Are you going to be a good boy?" An involuntary whine escaped my throat.

Pooley spoke up. "Is this really a good idea, Blythe?"

That's who the woman was: Blythe Pooley! Therm married her in law school. She came from money back East. Why was she in Hell? Why was everybody?!

Sammy hopped back in the truck and pulled away. Mrs Pooley stared at her husband and Stacey. They started to fidget.

"Did I lose the dog?"

"No, dear. I just meant—".

"Did I stand by and watch a deviant psychopath murder the most effective political pet in the entire Congress?"

"No, dear."

"No one—do you hear me?— *no one* is going to target you or any member of your household in a terrorist act.

"But someone just did—"

"No, Stacey—they did not. An unstable performance artist named Kerr had an accident and died in the Virginia mountains. That's all they've got. That and a damaged minivan, *completely empty*. Nothing that links any of us to that incident. You and Lucky weren't even there. We went over this."

"Believe me, if the three of us present this new dog to the world as Lucky, then I guarantee you: Lucky he will be."

I was dead—*and* I was a dog.

Pooley looked doubtful. "I'm not sure we should."

"Damn it, Therm—it's too late! We *removed evidence.*

She looked at the two of them and shook her head. "I wish I could fire you both." She got in her car and pulled out, leaving us in a cloud of annoyed dust.

Stacey bent down, trying to sound cheerful. "Well, Lucky—let's see if we can make the best of it, shall we?"

Pooley looked miserable. Why? He wasn't a dog.

"It'll be fun. We'll spend lots of time with the Frisbee and the duck dummies till nobody can tell the difference. Just the three of us, how's that sound?" She patted my side—which felt good—and we went inside.

I was Senator Pooley's dog. For two days I lived in denial. Pathetic—trying to walk on my back legs, shape words out of barks.... Each morning I'd try not to love the smell of the food in the dish marked "Lucky". But each afternoon the dish was empty.

At night I had the run of the house. It was mostly duck prints, plaid wallpaper, bass on a plaque. In the living-room though, there was one genuine work of art: a small sculpture by Giacometti. Its emaciated form, barely recognizable as human, haunted me. The Pooleys never even looked at it.

In the bathroom, I stared at myself in the full-length mirror. Lucky stared back. I thought of the reading I'd done, preparing for his abduction—knowledge that mocked me now. Dogs are descended from wolves. For twenty thousand years they were bred for specific traits—in general, for the appearance and behavior of puppies. Droopy ears, head and teeth smaller than a wolf's—and the persistent need never to grow up.

Wolves become self-sufficient, serious-minded, dangerous. Dogs become Peter Pan.

Neoteny. That's the scientific name for it. The persistence of juvenile characteristics into adulthood. A fitting fate, I thought, for an artist. So this was my hell. To be my enemy's dog.

(*A sudden revelation*) *My enemy's dog—?!* Good God, I thought—that's not Hell! I was in position to cause him the kind of pain and terror a mere artist could only imagine!

All the lights exploded in my head! I wasn't being punished! This was Heaven, not Hell! My reward, my opportunity. I was here to destroy Therm Pooley!

I ran upstairs and scratched at his door. Oh, don't be a sound sleeper! Stacey hurried from her room and led me back down. She moved around the house with such a proprietary air. I was going to have to find out how Mrs Pooley fit into all this.

"There you go, boy" Stacey said as she moved to shut my door. I whined—was that me?—and she hunkered down, rubbed my ears and kissed my forehead. "Don't be afraid, Lucky," she whispered, "Everything's going to be all right. The Senator just needs someone to rely on. That's you and me, ok?"

Her robe fell open. The moonlight rushed in to cover her. I stared at her breast. It swung, in a gentle, silvery arc, as unspeakably beautiful as I'd always known it must be. "I am a wall, and my breasts like towers..." She didn't close her robe. Why? I was a *dog.*

And suddenly the full weight of my transformation—the infinite barrier between me and this loveliest of women—crashed down. "Night, Lucky," she said, and the door slammed shut.

(*The ominous sound of distant howling*)

KERR: I fell into a deep, dream-encumbered sleep. Something was chasing me; something I couldn't see.

The next morning I leaped into my training. I picked up every trick they could teach. "Smartest dog I've ever seen," Pooley said. "It's like he knows exactly what I'm saying." I wagged my tail. I have no smile; I have a tail.

Stacey was working hard on Pooley. She was anxious about him; I could smell it. She called him Senator, praised his mediocre Frisbee tosses, but it was useless.

"How could a person do that, Stacey? Take an innocent dog—"

"Try to forget, Senator."

"I can't. Staring at this dog all the time. Damn spitting image."

"Should we take a little break? I know something else we could do."

She walked over and kissed him. I stared, open-mouthed. I'd always assumed this, of course—still...

(Watching them, KERR gives an involuntary wretching noise.)

KERR: Pooley wasn't in the mood. He shook his head and walked off, his mind far away.

(More low, distant howling)

KERR: That night, I lay dreaming. Something was chasing me, something with alcohol on its breath.

(As the howling fades out)

KERR: The door opened. In the dark I could barely make out the Senator in an oversized robe, staring at me. He reeked of bourbon. We went into his den. I hadn't been in this room before; the door was always shut. He

turned on the lamp, slumped in his chair and patted his
lap. "Come on, fella" he mumbled, "Jump on up."

I did as I was told, as every treacherous servant must.
With incredible delicacy he began to stroke the back of
my head. I'd been petted before. But this was the first
time he had touched me. It was...a revelation. This was
no sporty, romp-on-the-lawn, get-your-fur-all-mussed-
up kind of petting. This was the real stuff. The backs of
his fingers trailed loosely over my skull, following my
mid-line down over my neck—perfectly, effortlessly,
in touch with my innermost rhythms. Make no
mistake—this was a dog man.

"I'm not ready for this. Blythe's a pig in shit, of course.
She was scary enough as a congressman's wife. Now
I'm a senator."

He sighed. "Senator Therm Pooley. Therm. Thermal.
What the hell kind of name is that? Daddy said it'd be
good for politics—voter recognition. "'Good ol' Therm,
that's who I'm voting for!'"

He stopped petting me. I moved closer. Come on, come
on... He fixed on me. Who're you voting for, buddy?
You voting for ol' Therm?" I will if you scratch me.

I tried to look at him with moist-eyed devotion.
He began to weep. "God, I wish it was twenty years
ago. I got as beautiful a wife and personal assistant as
a man could want, and I don't want either one of 'em."
This was pretty nauseating, but he was petting me
again. My ears—he was doing the tips of my ears!

"Last night, right in the middle of things with Stacey,
I went limp. First time ever. At the crucial moment,
all I could think of was the forty-nine percent of the
electorate that voted against me. Forty-nine percent!"

He reached for a key and unlocked his desk drawer.
He pulled out a group of objects I instantly recognized.

They were from my van. There was the black hood,
the muzzle—oh God, there was Rat-cam!

"It's one thing not to vote for me," he mumbled,
"but this... Oh, Rat—you died for my sins, boy.
Clear as day". His hand went tight on my collar.
"Tell me, Lucky—who was Kerr? What kind of person
destroys not only your dog, but your self-confidence?"

Suddenly he pushed it all back in the drawer and
snapped on his computer. He pulled up a file called
"Justin." His correspondence with his son. Therm
began weeping again as he wrote.

"Dear Justin, We all hated military school at first.
I'm sorry about the rope burns you describe, but hazing
has always been part of the Academy. You will recover.
If things become truly intolerable, e-mail me
immediately. Love, Dad"

He read it over and pondered. "I don't know. Is that
what I should say?" He seemed to sigh his entire life
out. He leaned back in his chair and stared hopelessly
at the screen. His eyes closed. He started to snore.
I stretched my muzzle forward and sniffed the
computer. I used to be good with these. (Cautiously
putting out one "paw") If I just carefully...poked...
a key with my middle front claw...

And like magic, there it was! The unsent e-mail! I was
into the computer of Therm Pooley! I almost barked.
Fantastic! I could actually bring up a file! This felt so
good, so natural. And suddenly it hit me: of course
I was happy. I was retrieving! I looked at the letter
he'd written. I could modify it any way I wanted.

("Typing") "Dear Justin, I'm sorry I myself went to
military school. I wish I'd followed my first impulse
and become an artist. My chance is gone, you still have
time. E-mail me at once. I know of several fine dance
academies. Love, Dad"

And I sent it.

(Once again: low, distant growling)

KERR: That night I dreamed once again that something was chasing me. It was getting closer.

(The growling ends.)

KERR: The next morning, Therm took me for a walk. I loved walks. All night the smells of the world crept in under the laundry-room door. There was so much out there! Flowers, grass—sure, but the way the dirt smelled! One whiff and I pictured the last forty animals who'd been in and across it. This wasn't a sense, it was a superpower! I could smell beetles! Worms! The very body of the earth. And other smells, too. Three-week old urine—fantastic! Bird droppings, cow flop. Smells weren't good or bad anymore—they were like a library: filled with information. The sweat of people, horses, shit from other dogs, my own from yesterday! It was like some kind of endless movie that didn't have to have a plot. Image after image, animal after animal strode through my heart—each one firing off its own pure emotion. Fear, love, terror, love, nostalgia, amazement, love, love, love— Was there any other way to spend the day?!

We stopped in the middle of an empty field, at a small mound of dirt. The scent was faint but unmistakeable. Rat was buried here. Pooley stared down. "I'm sorry, Rat," he said, "Sorry we can't give you the monument you deserve. Wish you'd never jumped in to rescue that degenerate. But you were too well trained." I tried to work up some resentment, but just then a squirrel skittered by, and nothing else mattered. I strained at my leash. Therm pulled back angrily. "Damn it, Lucky! Settle down! It's only a squirrel!"

Only?!!

"You can't show any respect at all, can you boy? There never will be another Rat." Then he went on.

"Who knows when a marriage is over?" My ears pricked up. What was this about?

"Years before it breaks up, of course, but who can pinpoint the moment? Impossible. You just wake up one day knowing there's something you will never confide, a secret you will never trust her with. And you realize that she has a secret, too. Many perhaps. A new formality, a new carefulness creeps in. That's the moment you go into business together. It's not man and wife anymore, it's... partners. But you still have the secrets, and you have to tell 'em— some of 'em anyway. So you find Stacey—or a Stacey, some Stacey.

And she's fine for a secret or two. Loyal, hard-working, willing to go to bed with you, if you're up for it—which you're not. But you have more and more secrets. Finally you realize that only Rat can hear everything. Only Rat can be trusted. He knows what's in your heart the moment you walk in a room. His only desire is that you be there. There's something deep in his eyes—a place where you feel safe. He's more loyal to you than you are to yourself. That is the glory of a dog."

He looked at me. "Lucky? Can I trust you?".

I felt something that scared me to my core. I felt sorry for Therm Pooley.

(*A dog howls faintly in the distance.*)

KERR: That night, I couldn't get to sleep. I circled and circled on the little braid rug that served as my bed.

What was going on here? The more I was around Therm Pooley, the more I felt for him. It didn't make sense. I was here to bring the man down. Was this some kind of perverse spiritual test?

(*Slowly, the sound of a pack of wild dogs grows in the distance.*)

KERR: Suddenly, I stopped in my tracks. I lay flat and sniffed the fecund Maryland air. The same ghastly dream I had night after night came back to me, clear for the first time: running, an ocean of grass, my heart exploding, the hot breath of *whatever* on the back of my legs—! What kind of monster is this!? I looked back, and there it was—!!

(*The pack's barking crescendoes, then abruptly stops. In a terrified whisper*)

KERR: *The cutest little puppy in the world!*

I was terrified! My tongue soaked with sweat— what a *horrible* way to sweat! Neoteny! *Ne-ot-en-y!* That hideous, darling face of purest neoteny, doggedly running me to ground—

It hit me like a truck. The human consciousness I had taken so for granted was on its way out. Disappearing. Residual. (*In a desperate tone*) Vestigial!

(*A yip from a happy puppy.* KERR *looks horrified and quickly tumbles on.*)

KERR: I was going to be *all dog!* Soon, too. No wonder I liked being petted. No wonder the vagrant smells of the universe had begun to hold as much attraction for me as Futurist philosophy. This was a test, all right—a test with a time limit! I had to finish off the career of Therm Pooley, before I... I couldn't even say it—well, of course I couldn't *say* it.

All dog. All dog, all the time. Perpetual canine Alzheimer's. No tense but the present, no world but my yard. Nothing real unless it tastes like dinner, rubs up against me, floats up my nostrils—?

(*A restless, uncomfortable dog's whine*)

KERR: Once I was all dog, would I come to love Therm
Pooley? Would I lose all sense of morality, all—?
(*Suddenly realizing*) No...morality!? That shocked me
as deeply I could be shocked. No construct whatever
to place upon the world. *Only* the world? And no way
to have any idea that the world... *is?*

(KERR *moves once again the glass of water. He picks it up,
but instead of drinking like a human, he slurps like a dog. He
looks at the audience, embarrassed, and sets the glass down.*)

KERR: In the morning Senator Pooley went into his
study and locked the door. The annual debate on
funding the N E A was the next day, and his party
leaders wanted him to speak to charges that Kerr—
I mean, I—had been driven to suicide by his campaign
tactics. I whined at the keyhole as he worked on his
speech. Finally he let me in. I jumped into his chair.

"Down, boy. I'm working."

But I didn't get down. Instead, I stretched out my paw
and touched the keyboard.

"Hey, get away from—!"

Therm's voice died as he noticed the two letters I'd
struck happened to spell the word, "hi". He shook his
head and chuckled with just the slightest hint of unease.

"Well, I'll be. What the hell are the chances of a dog
doing that?"

I did it again. Pooley's eyes became perfect circles.

I did it again. His mouth opened like the drawbridge
of a surrendering medieval city.

I did it again. He turned the kind of white ashes become
just before they disappear.

He smelled afraid. That's an easy smell. But the odor
was accompanied by a strange new scent, which the
retriever in me instinctively recognized. It was the smell

of someone losing his mind. Vanilla—that was it.
It smelled exactly like vanilla extract. The aroma of
madness.

Therm pulled a second chair next to mine and sat
down. For a breathlessly long moment he stared at the
computer. Then he stared at me. He nodded almost
imperceptibly toward the screen. Again I typed "hi".

"Do you understand me?" he asked, in a voice like
glass.

I typed. "Yes."

The senator immediately got up and left the room,
shutting the door behind him. I thought about writing
him a letter, but decided to wait. A few seconds later
he returned.

"What's my name?"

"Senator Therm Pooley," I typed.

"Dear Jesus," he muttered.

This gave me a truly inspired idea.

I typed: "Please don't take my Master's name in vain."

He looked confused. "I'm your master," he said.

I typed again: "Only on Earth."

Pooley began to tremble. "Who are you?"

"The product of a miracle," I typed—which was true,
after all.

"A miracle of God?"

O K—some equivocations are bigger than others.
But let's face it: in the absence of evidence even for
the existence of God, any statement about His workings
has to be taken as at least conceivably true. Anyhow,
that's what I thought, so I typed "Yes".

The idea that I was a Christian miracle seemed to calm
Therm down a great deal. The vanilla odor quickly
dissipated. He fell to his knees; he began to pray out
loud. I felt embarrassed both as an intellectual and a
dog.

"Dear Lord, Help me understand why You have
sent your holy messenger to me. Give me the strength
to perform whatever tasks You may communicate
through him. Make me worthy Father, of this great
miracle."

Then he looked up at me with an expression few dogs
have seen on the face of a human: pure submission.

I turned and typed three little letters: "N E A".

He peered at the screen. "What do you mean, Lord?"

I had to straighten him out, if only to cover. I typed,
"I am not your Lord. The Lord is your Lord."

"I'm sorry. How do I address you?"

"You may call me Rat."

"Rat?! Is that you?!"

Time for some Christian mystery. "I am Rat. But I am
also much more. I am here to make you more perfect
in the eyes of God."

"May I...hug you?"

I could barely feel him, he held me so delicately. His
perfect moment—holding the one fellow creature he'd
ever loved, while at the same time embracing the love
which passeth all understanding. He seemed afraid
I'd evanesce in his arms, fly again to Heaven without
explaining the three letters hovering on his screen.
I went to the top of the document—the speech on the
N E A the Senator had been writing—and deleted it.

"I worked all morning on that—!"

"Sorry; it's heresy," I typed.

"It—? But...but what should I say?".

I decided to get Delphic. This had to feel like his idea.
I typed, "What is in your heart?"

"I make laws with my head, not my heart".

"God is love," I typed.

"Tough love maybe, if you're talking domestic arts
policy". "All love," I typed. I stared him straight in
the eye.

"What are you saying, that God *wants* us to have
federal support for the arts?"

Therm's voice was an incredulous whisper. "God wants
me to say *that*? On the Senate floor!?"

I licked his face. He really was very bright. Therm
stared at the blank screen. Pixels reflected merrily in the
beads of sweat on his upper lip. He couldn't possibly be
enough of a believer to throw an entire career away on
the word of one miraculous dog. And yet...

Suddenly he began to type: "Perhaps a longer-term
phaseout of the N E A—"

I gave a low growl. His hands jumped back.

"No?"

"*All* love," I typed. I could even underline.

"How could God ask this?" he murmured. Cautiously,
he typed again: "As an inexpensive gesture of solidarity
with the nations of Western Europe, a permanent if tiny
stipend for the arts—"

I put my paw gently on his hand.

"He wants more?"

I barked.

"I'm sorry. I'll get it; I really will."

Therm moved to the window and stared out.
The landscape stared back, no longer a familiar friend.
It was mysterious now—everything was. He sat down,
took a deep breath and tried one last time.

"The question before us—the only question in a
sense—is whether the national government has
the same right as any of its citizens: to love beauty
and challenge, to use its substance to promote and
perpetuate these qualities, and keep them from being
overwhelmed by the endless tide of the simply
profitable".

He looked anxious. "What do you think?"

I typed carefully. "God is pleased." I'm not entirely
atheistic. For all I knew there was a God. For all I knew
He was pleased.

Now that Therm knew which side God was on, he
turned out to be a stunningly good defender of federal
funding for the arts. He wrote a stirring defense of
the underlying concept, ancillary benefits to the public
and quite simply the essential goodness of extending
the right to possess an artistic dimension to as many
souls in our society as possible. I beat my tail against
the carpet. I ran in circles! I practically licked his ear off!

We were just about finished when a knock came.
"Not now!" Therm shouted.

"Lucky needs to go out. We don't want an accident,"
ventured a nervous Stacey.

She was right. I'd been so involved, I didn't realize
nature'd been calling for some time. As I groaned
with relief by the bush at the corner of the house,
I contemplated the mind of the Almighty, which I
decided must be very complex indeed. Sort of like a
compound insect eye—only more of a mental version?

You know, not that much focus on detail. Just this
phenomenal sweep of reality: big movements, bold
colors. Major trends. Maybe that's what I was—a whole
new trend. Maybe every politician would now have a
miraculous pet, dedicated to his downfall. Maybe I
was part of an enormous, planned improvement.

Just then I caught a strange and troubling scent.
Automatically, I followed it and discovered a—
and here I use the technical term—mixed bitch.
A broken leash trailed from her collar. Clearly a
runaway. And clearly, I regret to say, in heat.

I started to quiver. This was the last thing I wanted
to think about. But it was getting harder to conjure
thoughts of the Deity. Why was she whimpering like
that? I had to ignore her. Therm'd be lost without his
sacred messenger— Did she like me? I didn't care!
I had other things to— Man! That scent was distracting!
She could've been a pit bull or a Pomeranian—or a
mountain goat, for that matter! All I wanted to do
was—no! No! What was I—some kind of animal? Yes!
Yes!! I was some kind of animal! Some kind, anyway.
I mean, why not? Just WHY THE HELL NOT!!?
And suddenly I was on her! I couldn't help it!
I used to be very big on foreplay, but not anymore, boy!
You couldn't've stopped me with a sledgehammer!
Don't misunderstand—she was obviously all for it.
I mean, why not? I was *terrific!* And for the first time
it was so...so...*uncomplicated!!*

Just then Therm Pooley, speech in hand, came around
the corner. He stared in disbelief. I was shocked—
I didn't stop, but I was definitely shocked.

"What in HELL—!!?"

He just stood there, staring. Did he have *no* sense of
privacy? Excuse me, I'm in the middle of something
here!

"Stop it, Lucky! Stop it right now!" He reached for
my collar, but I snapped at him. *Hey!!* Don't even *think*
about it!

Stacey came around the corner. Oh great—let's sell
tickets!

"Senator? Your wife's on the pho—oh, *God!!* That's the
Andersons' dog! What's she—!? She's just a mutt!"

Oh, yeah—and you're so highly pedigreed.

Therm was white with rage. "You pervert! You...you
false prophet! You dare call yourself a *messenger of
God?!*"

Stacey looked at him funny.

Just then God sent one of His most popular messages.
I delivered it faithfully to my female counterpart.
She, at least, was overjoyed. Stacey took hold of her
and headed toward the Andersons'.

So, what was it you wanted?

Clutching his speech, Therm started inside. I barked.
He gave a cold stare. "How could you—? What...
what *are* you?!"

He locked himself in the study again—this time
without me. All day calls came in. Everyone wanted
to know what was in his speech, but he was
incommunicado. I listened at the door. The ominous
sound of keystrokes and mumbled prayers plagued my
soul. Do dogs have souls, I wondered? Do bad dogs?

Blythe was going particularly nuts. In the evening she
drove out from Washington, but by then Therm had
sneaked out of the house and disappeared. All he left
was a note on his desk that said, "I want everyone in
the Gallery tomorrow—*especially* Lucky—or I'll cede
my time to Ted Kennedy".

The Senate Gallery was crowded. The debate over eliminating the N E A had grown into a new national art form. Therm's party loved it: humiliation, pure and simple.

I had to pretend I was a seeing-eye dog, which meant Stacey had to wear dark glasses. While the majority leader spoke, Senator Pooley sat at his desk, staring straight ahead.

"I heard from Justin this morning," Blythe muttered. "He read me an utterly irrational e-mail from his father. E-mail is *not secure*, Stacey. Neither is Therm, if he screws this up".

"Yesterday he called Lucky...a false prophet," Stacey said.

"He what?!"

"I'm sure it was just a joke."

Therm walked to the podium. I noticed a shape in his coat pocket.

It looked almost like...like...

"What's that? What's in his pocket?" Blythe hissed at Stacey.

"I don't know".

"Did you check his gun safe last night?"

"I thought you did".

"Oh, my God!"

We watched breathlessly as he arranged the papers. Had he snapped? I sniffed the air for vanilla extract—but there was such a cloud of it in there! Who could tell?

Therm looked up—right at us, stared for one of those infinite moments and began.

"An artist named Kerr, whom some of you may know, died recently in the mountains of Virginia. Kerr..." He paused for a torturously long moment. The whole room leaned forward—I was glad I was already on all fours.

"Kerr...was made by the same God who made me. But that God chose to give Kerr a burden. The burden was to love, above all things, that which surprised and resonated in the human heart."

The color drained from Blythe's cheeks.

"We drive our cars, make our deals, raise our children— we whistle our happy tunes. Each day we go through life as though we know what life is. But we don't know what life is. We know *that* it is, and we know that it ends. But what life is has been debated since life began."

"He's lost his mind," Blythe muttered.

"Are there miracles in life?" He looked up at me. I barked; I couldn't help it.

"I for one know that there are. And because I know this, I recognize that there are dimensions of life that we do not understand, that we must explore. If we refuse to do this, if we fail to examine publicly and persistently and collectively the innermost nature of life we lose the right to call ourselves a society at all. We become merely an aggregation of purposeless spirits, ghosts encased in flesh."

The majority leader whispered frantically with colleagues. Beyond that, the entire room was still.

Therm's hand went into his pocket. Blythe ducked. Stacey gave a short, terrified scream. Carefully he pulled out not a gun, but the little Giacometti from their living room—which no one had even noticed was missing. He set it on the podium and delicately ran a finger along it.

"Nearly two hundred years ago we sent Lewis and
Clark to go where we could not. To explore a land
we knew was ours, but which only they could reach.
They brought it back to us. I would submit that a
similar land, but far vaster, occupies the human soul.
Only a few people—those who have dedicated
themselves, people like Kerr—can find the way there.
If we help them go we help ourselves, because they
can—they will—bring it back to us. Their discoveries
won't all be happy or beautiful. Some will be
dangerous. But each will enlarge us. Deepen us.
Revive us. The money they ask is pitiful. In relative
terms, we paid more for Manhattan Island—"

I heard a thump. It was the majority leader. He'd
crumbled to the floor only a few feet from the podium,
clutching his chest. He was having a heart attack—
or one of the most convincing fake heart attacks of
all time. His face was like blue granite. Instantly
the floor was awash with senators, security guards,
paramedics—my God, they must keep them under
the desks!

Blythe couldn't take her eyes off the Giacometti that
lingered in Therm's hand. "Dear God," she said,
"It looks like an Oscar for failing".

We all rode back to the farm together, in complete
silence. What was there to say? I myself would never
forget Therm Pooley's greatest moment. Amazing what
was in him all along, just waiting to be shaken out of
his unconscious: a ruby fallen from the sheets of an
unnamed guest.

Sure there was the aroma of vanilla in the car, but there
was also genuine growth. That part smelled like used
Legos.

There were news vans at the front gate when we
arrived. We drove straight to the house. Blythe and
Stacey spoke, then confronted Therm.

"Honey?" Blythe carefully began, "Stacey's going to
take you over to Doc Maynes." Doc Maynes was an old
friend and confidante who lived on the Eastern Shore.
He was also a psychotherapist.

"I don't need to see Doc Maynes."

"If you want to stay married, you do. Stacey will take
you in the boat. Don't want the reporters to know
where you're going."

"Then Lucky's going, too."

A boat ride? That sounded great. I had the irrational
feeling—maybe not for a dog—that a boat ride would
make us all feel just...I don't know...fabulous!

(Sound of a boat's engine)

KERR: Stacey handled the boat. Therm stared out at the
high reeds along the reach. Marsh all around. It looked
like my dream.

We sped straight out into open water. On and on
we went. When we couldn't see land anymore, Stacey
cut the engine, sat astride the Senator's lap and kissed
him deeply. What was with these people? Did all sex
require an audience?

She stood, pulling him with up her. Finally their kiss
broke. She said, "I have something for you".

And before he could ask, "What?" she pushed him into
the bay.

Tears streamed from her gleaming eyes as she restarted
the engine. "Stacey!" he yelled, "Wait—*what are you
doing!!?*"

We pulled away.

"STACEY—!!!"

She stopped again. We were hailing distance from him now.

"I'm doing this for you!"

"For me!!?"

"You're not stable! If you die in an accident, Blythe can take your place!"

"What are you talking about!!?"

"There'll be a special election! Blythe says widows always win!"

"What's she paying you? I'll triple it!!"

She was petting me now, better than she ever had.

"I'm not doing this for money! I'm doing it for your principles! They must be protected at all costs! You said so yourself, in your speeches—!"

"What about today's speech, Stace?! What about that?!"

"That wasn't you." She petted me even better.

"Lucky! *Lucky—save me!* Come on, boy—save your master!"

"We're miles out! He'd just drown too!"

She was probably right. I'd never seen so much water. And the way she was stroking my chin—

"SAVE ME, LUCKY—!!"

Let him go, I thought. I died for him; God knows he can return the favor. The Futurists always played for keeps; why shouldn't I? A fitting end for one who'd made his career on the politics of exclusion: betrayed by everyone closest to him, even by his dog.

"LUCKY—!!!"

This is not a movie, Therm Pooley. This is performance
art. Life and death. You never understood that—but
you do now.

His head went under. He popped up again, gasping.
Stacey held me close.

"LUCK-Y—!!!!"

It was his last shout. His last chance to cry out against
the universal injustice of death. He stared me in the eye,
unbelieving. Then he was gone.

*(From offstage comes the distant, inconsolable howling of a
dog)*

KERR: I started to howl. I don't know why. It was the
sheer loneliness of it! Dogs are pack animals—to be
separated is torture. *(A whisper of terror)* He was gone!
I thought I'd feel elation—but this was terrifying.
Where was he? Why wasn't he here? *Where was Therm
Pooley?!!* I couldn't stop panting. The silence of the
water overwhelmed me. I'd never had an anxiety attack
this bad—even as an artist. Even that first night, with
the first audience, wondering what made me wander
onto a stage of all places, as though I had anything to
give them. As though anyone has anything to give
anybody. As though we aren't all locked in a cell
of our own uniqueness with no doors, no windows,
formulating our own idiosyncratic code to tap uselessly
on the walls—!

I jumped. I fought my way out of the warmth of
Stacey's arms and...jumped.

Why? Therm Pooley wasn't worth saving. Just because
he could be manipulated through primitive religious
belief to do what he should have done out of simple
good sense? It wasn't enough. Still, I jumped.

Maybe it was the sensual thrill of the water itself.
My God, I was born for this!

I swam to the point we'd last seen him and dived
down. My gaze stabbed left and right until—I saw
him! Unconscious, dangling in the sunlit bay.

I took his sleeve between my teeth and started hauling.
The climb was slow. At last we broke the surface.
Stacey and the boat were nowhere to be seen. I looked
at Therm—he wasn't breathing.

I bit him. Hard. I didn't know what else to do. Mouth
to mouth was clearly out. I bit harder. Suddenly he
screamed—coughing, spluttering—but alive!
"Lucky—? Are you—? Did you—? *Where's Stacey?!!*"

As he took in the full circle of the horizon his face
turned absolutely historical. His eyes closed; he went
limp.

The easiest way to tow him was by his jacket front.
I took hold of him and swam in the direction that
smelled most like shore. Hour after hour went by,
mile after silent mile. Still no land.

I started feeling sleepy. Even as I kept swimming,
my eyes fell shut, the dream beginning. Time began
to lose its shape. Maybe I'd been swimming forever,
maybe I would swim forever more. Could that be hell
for a Chesapeake Bay Retriever? An endless supply
of what I loved most?

Then—suddenly—my paws were touching land!
Impossible! My eyes flew open—it was all around!
Incredible! Shore! Trees! Chirring insects, angry
blackbirds—dirt everywhere! Dirt, dirt, dirt!

I started biting Therm again until he woke up.
"Where are we?" his eyes seemed to be saying.
I looked around. A few yards down the beach was
something unbelievable. For a moment I wondered if
this truly was a post-mortem delusion—or in my case,
post-post-mortem.

Standing in sublime isolation in this marshy wilderness
was the fishing shack I had rented for the summer.
And this is when I knew there was a God. For while the
ways were mysterious, yet they were shapely, and the
remnant of my artist's soul rejoiced. Therm broke the
window and let us in. The stores I'd left were still there.
He dried us off with a towel, found new clothes, then
opened a can of tuna for him and one of Science Diet
for me. We ate quietly on the front step, staring as the
late afternoon light streaked across the illimitable bay.

After a long time, Therm pulled the Giacometti out of
his pocket. He started to scratch with it in the moist
sand at our feet. He was writing. I cocked my head
to read:

"Thank you for saving my life."

My paw scratched in the sand before me:

"O K."

He wrote again: "I don't mean from drowning."

I wrote, "I know."

He scratched, "Is there anything you want to tell me?"

"Yes," I wrote, "I'm not really the messenger of God."

He wrote: "Who are you?"

"I'm Kerr."

He stared a long time out at the water. Then he wrote:
"You may be God's messenger and not know it."

I wrote: "You've got a point there."

He wrote: "I don't know if I can be comfortable
with Kerr for my dog."

I wrote: "I'm changing. Soon Kerr won't exist.
I'll only be Lucky."

"Does that make you sad?"

"No. Kerr lived a good life."

"Yes," Therm wrote. "Yes, he did". Then Therm wrote a lot. He wrote: "It's taken twenty-thousand years for men and dogs to form their relationship. In all that time, have they done anything else nearly as well?"

I wrote, "Not even close."

We didn't write any more after that. That night, as we slept in the cabin, Therm's snores comforted me. I was ready for the dream-chase through the tall weeds this time. Ready for the heart of the puppy finally to contain my heart. Neoteny—the miracle of childish good will never abandoned. By the time summer is through, we will fashion for ourselves new names and friendlier faces, and—with no other weapons but these—walk back into the world.

THE END

REPRODUCTION

CHARACTERS

HARRIET, *seventeen, large and pregnant*
MOOZIE, *seventeen, small and pregnant*
NATHAN, *seventeen, in jeans*
JOHN, *seventeen, in a jacket and tie*

HARRIET: I was fat to start. I felt fat. Actually, I was thin. But I was so big and thin and ugly that I felt fat. My Mom thinks that I got knocked up so I could really be fat. I don't know why I got knocked up. It happened the first time I ever did it. Not the first time. More like the fifteenth time. The boy was a virgin. Really. He cried when it was over. He shouldn't have. My Dad is dead. Which is lucky, 'cause he would've killed him. My Mom's alive. Sort of. She didn't make me leave the house or anything, once I got knocked up. She just stopped talking to me. So, I went to a home for knocked-up girls. Sat on the step till my Mom had to give up and put me in it. When she left me there, she finally said something to me. She said I slept with boys 'cause I couldn't hold up my end of a decent conversation.

MOOZIE: I'm so small that when my baby's born it'll probably kill me. That's what I hope, anyway. It's not that I want to die, it's that I want to die for something. That baby would be here because of me, because of what I did. 'Course they'll probably take it out by Caesarean anyway. Which won't help anybody, since either way it'll be alive, only this way no one will have sacrificed anything—not even pain, I'll be under anesthetic. I'm not complaining or anything, don't get me wrong. I was just hoping my baby would have something special to start its life with. Like a human sacrifice. That sounds awful, doesn't it? I don't mean it like that. I mean like heroes in war movies or doctors in epidemic movies. When they die. Human sacrifices. It's O K to be a sacrifice as long as you have very specifically in mind what you're doing at all times, *and* who's going to live on. Then I think it can be quite beautiful.

NATHAN: I don't have any opinion one way or the other
about abortion. I'm a man, and so it'd be pretty stupid I
think to pull some holier-than-woman act out of my hat
and say yes you can or no you can't. 'Cause as a man
I think you're always there by invitation, you know?
It's no good if you're not. I mean, what kind of a jerk
are you if you trick your way in, or if you...force your
way in, or.... No matter what, you have to be invited.
So. I don't have opinions about abortions and things.
My girl does. She's going to have the baby. Actually,
she's not my girl. She's... we dated. Twice. And, you
know how you sometimes get embarrassed to ask about
contraception when you're going to bed with a person?
And so you don't ask? And they weren't using any?
So they get pregnant? So you're a father? She wants to
get married. I told her I hardly knew her. She says she
doesn't care. I told her how many lives do you want to
ruin here, anyway? She got a real funny smile on her
face and said, just yours.

JOHN: I saw a documentary on the reproductive cycle of
cuckoos. It was really fascinating. You see, they don't
make nests. They lay their eggs in the nests of little
warblers, in the reeds of a swamp. They wait till the
warblers are out singing or something, and then they
come down like a big blimp and drop this elephant-
sized egg, and leave. When the warblers come back,
they start to take care of this egg—along with their own
eggs. The big egg, the cuckoo egg, always hatches first.
And the warbler parents feed this baby cuckoo, just like
he was one of their own. They feed him and feed him,
and real soon he's as big as they are. Well, about then
the warbler babies hatch out. Three or four of them.
Little...warblers. And this very big other baby, this
cuckoo, has like a groove built into its back? Something
nature put there? For every cuckoo. Anytime the
cuckoo feels something touch this groove on its back,
it pushes and pushes till that thing is gone instinctively.
So when the warbler parents are out looking for worms
and the warbler babies bump against the cuckoo's back,
he pushes them all out of the nest, one by one. They fall
down and break their necks or starve or get eaten by
a snake. They die before their eyes are even open. He
kills them before *his* eyes are open. When the warbler
parents get back, they don't even notice. They feed the
cuckoo till he gets big as a Buick, and then he just flies
away. It's the perfect crime. Of course it's not a crime.
Nobody knows what he's doing. All that murder in the
dark isn't murder at all. Just a bunch of jostling around,
wondering what life is, and then finding out. I told
my girlfriend about that show. She said if Original Sin
really exists, there must be a cuckoo in every corner of

Hell. I said nothing's a sin if you don't know it's a sin.
She said everything's a sin if you don't even get to open
your eyes.

HARRIET: The night I got knocked up, we did it in the dark. I never do it in the dark. He was embarrassed, though. Didn't want me to see his...whatever it was. Like I say, when it was over he cried. You know how everybody wonders what it was like when they got conceived? That's how it was. Dark, with the T V on in the other room. Him crying and saying I'm sorry I'm sorry I'm sorry. I haven't seen him since. Don't want to. I like the other girls here at home. There's twelve of us, and we're all knocked up—like that's the normal way to be and everybody else is odd. It's kind of a relief. Twelve little stupid babies nobody meant to have. Twelve girls who wouldn't know how to be mothers if their lives depended on it. Mostly we just act like twelve girls—hang out, smoke when we can, get mad about no privacy. We nod a lot when the counselors talk. Some of us listen. The rest of us know it doesn't matter. Last week, one of the girls had a miscarriage. She had to go home. I don't think she cared about the kid so much. What really got her was leaving us, having to go back to her folks. At first she said she was going to kill herself. Then she said she was going to get knocked up again, and come back. Doctor told her it'd be dangerous, of course. But she needed the friends.

MOOZIE: Maybe you didn't quite understand what I
meant about human sacrifices. I don't believe in death
for death's sake. I think that would be self-defeating.
What I really believe in is sort of life and death killing
each other, that's really the conventional view. You
know—death ending life, life ending death. Mom won't
listen to me anymore when I talk about this. In fact
nobody will, but I think it's very important. I mean,
throughout a person's life there's death *and* life—like
for instance, there are things that make me feel dead
even when I'm breathing. It's a strange sensation. Sort
of like being in a whole room covered with terry cloth.
You know—everything's inoffensive, an O K color, easy
to wash. But...it's terry cloth. In fact, that's why I got
pregnant. 'Cause I was feeling like I was in this terry
cloth room all the time. My Mom really does use terry
cloth. She puts slip covers on everything. I was getting
afraid she'd make a terry cloth slip cover for me.
I decided it was 'cause she thought I was like the
furniture. So I got pregnant. Thought I'd give her
a problem. I know that's bad. But I think good and
bad are two interesting concepts, too...just like life
and death. I told Mom all this and she said it was just
wonderful I was so smart and pregnant. I told her
smart girls had a right to get pregnant, too. She didn't
really have an answer for that. She just went back to
making clothes for the baby. Out of terry cloth.

NATHAN: The girl that's going to have my kid is named
Diane. The girl I'm going with is Bonnie. The girl I
really want to go out with is named Sandy. Sandy's
incredible. She has this way of stopping in a
conversation and just looking at you, you know?
Like looking ought to be enough? And usually, I mean,
with her, it is. She's been going out with someone else
though, so I haven't done anything. I talk about her a
lot. You know, to Bonnie and Diane. I know I shouldn't.
They get pretty mad, too. But.... Anyway, last night she
called me up. Really. Out of the blue. Said this is Sandy.
I said, yeah? She said she wondered what I was doing
later, and said did I want to hit a movie? I said, ok. Said
she'd be over in ten minutes. I felt pretty good. Then
right after I put the phone down, it rang again. It was
Bonnie—you know, the girl I'm going with? She said I
had to come over right away. I said, I can't, but she said
Diane's over here. You know, the one who's... I said
what's she doing there? I mean, Diane and Bonnie
pretend each other's not alive. Bonnie said she didn't
know why Diane was there, but she was sitting in the
living room and she was crying and she had a knife.
And could I please come over. I left Sandy a note and
got the hell over. Bonnie's folks were gone, and sure
enough there was Diane with this big, scary-looking
kitchen knife that actually wasn't half as scary as the
way her eyes looked. She was sitting on the couch, just
staring at the knife. I said, Hi Diane, how's it going? But
she didn't say anything. Bonnie tried to shove me more
into the room, but I wasn't going to get anywhere near
that knife. I told Bonnie—you know, real quiet—I told
her we should call nine-one-one. She said what's that? I

said nine-one-one, nine-one-one goddammit—haven't
you ever had an emergency? And she said, I can't have
an emergency in my folks' house. And I started moving
toward the kitchen for the phone, and Bonnie stuck
right with me, saying, we can't call the police, this is my
folks' house. And I started to dial the phone and Bonnie
pulled the cord out of the phone and stuck it down the
garbage disposal and turned it on and chopped the
cord all up to hell. And I said how are you going to
explain *that* to your folks? And she said get her out of
this house right now, you stupid pig. And I let that go,
and we both went back around the other way, you
know, to sneak up on her a little—and when we turned
the last corner and looked in on Diane—she wasn't
there anymore. There was just a note instead, lying
next to the knife. It said, "You deserve each other."

JOHN: There's a group of echinoderms which are
known as holoturians. That means they're not like
starfish or anything. They're—well, they are what they
are—they're sea cucumbers. And they're animals like
everybody else, but they—some of them—actually do
look a little like cucumbers. They float around in the
ocean you know, and...don't do much. I tried to tell
my girl about them, but she thinks nature's evil, for
the most part. Anyway, there's nothing really about
sea cucumbers that's interesting. Except this one thing.
If something—like a fish—actually bites them, or gets
too close, the sea cucumber will jettison part of its own
internal organs—you know, like its intestines and
things—and shoot them out—and then swim away.
The fish eats the stuff that got jettisoned, and the sea
cucumber escapes. The sea cucumber can even
regenerate those same internal organs later. Really.
Well, this is about how far I got telling my girl about it.
Then she said if I ever tried to tell her about nature
again she'd vomit in my shoes. She won't sleep with
me. I want her to, but she says nature is the prime evil
in the universe, and the planets worth living on are the
ones that don't have any. She says the less connection
she has with nature the happier she's going to be. I said
what if we want babies someday? She said all she wants
are pretend babies. I said, shoot, you might as well be
forty-five right now. She said, thank you, that is my
ambition. Then we had some pretend sex. She said
we'd made a pretend baby. I said how could you know
that? She said she could feel it inside. She said it felt
good, and comfortable, and secure. She liked the idea

that it could stay there forever, that it could never be born.

BROADWAY PLAY PUBLISHING INC

PLAYS WITH MORE WOMEN THAN MEN

BESIDE HERSELF

A BRIGHT ROOM CALLED DAY
(IN PLAYS BY TONY KUSHNER)

CHURCH OF THE HOLY GHOST

DAME LORRAINE
(IN PLAYS BY STEVE CARTER)

A DARING BRIDE
(IN PLAYS BY ALLAN HAVIS, VOLUME TWO)

GOONA GOONA

THE LADIES OF FISHER COVE
(IN PLAYS BY ALLAN HAVIS, VOLUME TWO)

MINK SONATA
(IN PLAYS BY ALLAN HAVIS)

ONLY IN AMERICA
(IN PLAYS BY AISHAH RAHMAN)

BROADWAY PLAY PUBLISHING INC

PLAYS WITH MORE WOMEN THAN MEN (CONT'D)

ON THE VERGE

PECONG

PHANTASIE

RAIN. SOME FISH. NO ELEPHANTS.

SHOW AND TELL
(IN PLAYS BY ANTHONY CLARVOE)

STARSTRUCK

STONEWALL JACKSON'S HOUSE

UNFINISHED WOMEN CRY IN A NO MAN'S LAND WHILE A BIRD DIES IN A GILDED CAGE
(IN PLAYS BY AISHAH RAHMAN)

WHAT A MAN WEIGHS

BROADWAY PLAY PUBLISHING INC

LONG ONE ACTS
(WRITTEN WITHOUT AN INTERMISSION)

BAL
(IN PLAYS BY RICHARD NELSON
EARLY PLAYS VOLUME TWO)

BEIRUT
(IN PLAYS BY ALAN BOWNE)

BETWEEN EAST AND WEST

THE BEST OF STRANGERS
(IN FACING FORWARD)

FLOOR ABOVE THE ROOF

FLOOR SHOW: DOÑA SOL AND HER TRAINED DOG
(IN PLAYS BY EDWIN SÁNCHEZ)

HAITI (A DREAM)
(IN FACING FORWARD)

HARM'S WAY

**THE HELIOTROPE BOUQUET BY SCOTT JOPLIN & LOUIS
CHAUVIN**

HOLY DAYS

HOUSE OF SHADOWS
(IN PLAYS BY STEVE CARTER)

ICARUS